# WHERE THE
# FLOWERS GROW

# WHERE THE FLOWERS GROW

ALEX VELLIS

REBEL SATORI PRESS

*New Orleans & New York*

Published in the United States of America by
Rebel Satori Press
www.rebelsatoripress.com

Cover Art:

Paperback ISBN: 978-1-60864-399-8
eISBN: 978-1-60864-400-1

# Contents

## Introduction:

All the poems are named in accordance with 'The Language of Flowers: An Alphabet of Floral Emblems (London; New York: T. Nelson and Sons, 1857)'.

I started writing 'where the flowers grow' in 2019 when I was getting my MA in Creative Writing from the University of Kent. The following year, the world collapsed… and it hasn't really improved.

However, this collection, for me at least, is a triumph. This is six years of writing, editing, starting over, giving up, and continuing. In a lot of ways, this book is about metamorphosis, liminality, and the queer experience; as told by both a bisexual person and an agender person inhabiting the same shell.

A few of the boys that are written about in these pages are no longer with us, and this book is my dedication to them. I miss them every day and I hope they have found happiness now.

I hope you take something away from these poems, carry them with you, and find new homes for them in your life.

# Butterfly Orchid

My bed is beneath a bay window
& I have fucked everyone I know on it.

The romantic idea of a bay window
disintergrates when you see the mattress
on the floor.
                    I am in my twenties
& move around like I have magnetic blood.
|bed frames do not fit in a suitcase|

so we fuck wherever I lay the cushions
& you tell me this is fine.

We read each other love poems & point
fingers at world maps of past conflagrations.

We talk of Paris like a wet dream
|fluid//unplanned|
– & I am inside you.

Beneath the bay window, we are royalty,
both barons & barren

unlikely to be fed again.
We are gouged
by the kids that never made it; hot handprints
on unclean glass, telling our father's lies.

## Barberry

eyes scanning
trying to figure out
how much I pay for my haircut
                              'who are ya'
the door swings open

pulsing a nursery rhyme

the engine of the pub
roars as tables lose their footing
& madmen
become close-quarter enemies
before settling back down

in the cubicle men share
secrets kept from their wives
& touch hands for a second

he looks me up and down
like there's nothing
he wants                on the menu
    this could be an abattoir

he says

"I ain't seen you 'ere b'fore"

I say

"'eard this the best flat beer in

Britain"

he laughs washing his hands of sweat & piss

& me

# Cypress

On the roadside lies a dying cow
hit by a lorry, turned inside out
but still breathing – I walk to its side, cautiously,
kindly, not to get too close      kneel next to it & stroke
its head, out of the way of its broken legs, still kicking
in the hot sun    It croons out in misery & I join it
whilst I look for a rock big enough      We cry
together for different reasons both aware
of what comes next

## Heliotrope

It is my first time in a club – I am eighteen years old
really I am sixteen years old but the men in the queue
hear *six* as *eight* & I don't correct them.
An older man in his thirties looks me up & down
strapping me under his arm, running his fingers across my ribs
like strings on an instrument, we kiss, one of those long, slow kisses
that feels like the sins of the father were committed for us.
The bouncer eagles my soft skin against the leather of the man
& ushers us both inside. Under the black light of the club,
all the seats are zebra print – bodies splayed out in Grecian poses,
burying away from the sun. We grew as hard as bone on the
dancefloor, grinding our cocks to dust against denim & spandex &
vinyl. At the bar, I order gin & tonic, what my mother drinks – to
prove I deserve to be there; pink gin to show my adolescence – to
signify that I am not a predator, that I am prey, that I want to be
preyed on.

The hungry eyes on the dancefloor
call me & I gyrate a mating call

        – in the hands of Gods, we are all children –

searching for love, lost sheep trying to return to a shepherd – this field is thirsty, dry, & looking to swallow this flock whole, if we let it, it will eat us alive.

I search for phone numbers on the back of men's teeth & let my hips make decisions in the thrum of the bassy Latin rhythms. I have found life for the first time, sweaty, starving life on the cusp of a dancefloor, at the bar, where two men discover what they are for the first time that night, where all men wear make-up & look gorgeous, where our fathers roll over in their graves whether they are dead or not, where we are all gay best friends, where toilets are for fucking, & dancefloors are for fucking, & the bar is for rehydrating before we get back to fucking – where voyeurism is not a choice – & ravenous mouths will feed on youth before the night ends.

The club, an emptying bastion, has guard dogs – older men with bellies full of rum, holding their stiletto knives by the heel. Walking us in groups of four or so to the taxi rank before returning to collect the next bouquet of men. In the early morning, the evening turns to stone, & we hold each other close. Tomorrow will see us forgetting
each other's names but for tonight, we have every story we've ever known spilling from soft liquid lips.

# Eglantine

what does he hide     when he's alone
that I don't    in an open mouth
his neck breaks     looking back
in the wrong places    swallowing poetry
he wrote    when he was a kid
terrible & uninspired   much like everything else
journal entries    made of clay
in the softest way       harden him
as a path out of the dark    he sheds his layers
clothes & skin drop   pennies in a well
counting teeth on the way     down & out of sight
I have always been alive   somewhere in the water
in the depths of a cave   carefully constructed out of parts
       smoking cigarettes   as a fashion statement
waiting for something   that wants to speak
to crawl out of my mouth    into yours

# Red Bay

On the bottom bunk

　　　　　　　　　　two boys discover
　　　　　　　　　　what diaspora means:
explorers for the first time. Here, everything smells
like fresh linen & body sweat.

On the bottom bunk
two boys disappear
buried under the weight
of a blanket cave-in – they are miners, excavators, & heavy
like water on a grave.

On the bottom bunk

　　　　　　　　　　two boys destroy
　　　　　　　　　　each other
wrecking balls swinging into poorly built bodies
too young to understand change.

On a bench

　　　　　　many years later
　　　　　　they will see
　　　　　　each other

for the first time
since the last time
& they will know
each other
by the bruises.

## Sweet Sultan

thisisanotherletteriwillneversend
hisisanotherletteriwillneversend
isisanotherletteriwillneversend
sisanotherletteriwillneversend
isanotherletteriwillneversend
sanotherletteriwillneversend
anotherletteriwillneversend
notherletteriwillneversend
otherletteriwillneversend
therletteriwillneversend
herletteriwillneversend
erletteriwillneversend
rletteriwillneversend
letteriwillneversend
etteriwillneversend
tteriwillneversend
teriwillneversend
eriwillneversend
riwillneversend
iwillneversend
willneversend
illneversend

llneversend

lneversend

neversend

eversend

versend

ersend

rsend

send

sent

# *Marigold*


The sound between two points is an echo.
Echoes carry souvenirs like messenger birds.
Messenger birds suffocate in the hand.
The hand is a cemetery.


I spoke in your voice so that it would return
to me the love I missed. It gave me back
my own voice, softer than before.


The sound between two points is an echo.
Echoes carry souvenirs like messenger birds.
It gave me back my own voice, softer than before.
Your voice is a cemetery.

# Cedar Leaf

We are two men                         holding each other
more or less                           down on a bed
dressed in hand-me-downs               ex-lovers names not spoken
from our mothers – trying              to recall current lover's name
not to look like our fathers           instead we look to each other
trying not to wear stubble             bristled face pressed to bristled face
on nights out we are queens            here we are two bodies gorging
lacy & silken & feared                 on each other's fingertips
fingers wrapping champagne              pouring down each other's chests
vodka soda & lime                      drowning on the bedside cabinet
light tearing apart the dance          in the morning coffee hours
floor slutty in our heels    a harem of clothes sits quiet in the room
dogs being ordered to wait    before we have to go back to our lives

## Purple Columbine

this hole of pins
in the palm of my hands
stitching a smile
wide open

we are new
in our nakedness
fresh-faced & alive
bottle cap eyes on
the nightstand
a place for prayer
thrown across the room
during the fire we started
as kindling

a flower carved
between bed sheets
wanting & immortal
I collect you in glass jars
& ask if you had a name
you told me not before tonight

an itch
soldering metal
bearing teeth
to see my name

fresh leaves raked
against our skin
in the name of Gods with
bed frame bodies
a collection of memories
that knew how to behave
an impossible quiet
lies down to sleep
as children

a river made of hands
enshrined in sweat
clean & sweet
dug out of the sea
sprawled across your tongue
calling into the salted air

## Wild Geranium

I was hungry to have God in my mouth
         to feed my body what it needs
in each stolen evening; a firefly waltzing
         the grandeur of your voice
this thing inside of me – buried in my hands
         scratching at the corners of my lips
in all the places I had forgotten how to wash
         making me feel fuckable again
against the gentle ebbing of your body
         the mattress roaring into life
this infernal machine; a captor on raised legs
         now a celebration of names
dictating the angles of your body in the room
writing you & I into biblical texts
losing our skin between each other
         tasting our come on each other
burying our hands in shapes we had forgotten how to make
         till our bodies bleed as one
& our gasps for breath are no longer medical
         sleep deprived & happy
singing each other into prayer; hymns as doctrine
         making names for ourselves where we can

## Field Anemone

the sins of our parents
are bruises hidden under
our shirts growing red
& blue flowers
for teenagers who come home
too late from school

entire lives are remembered
on the scars on our wrists
languages we learned
telling each other that even
from different houses
we had the same family

our history begging on street'
corners hiding under staircases
silent in the volcanic tempers
of our fathers now too old
to say sorry are sold back to us
by therapists promising freedom

this is a war cry
from a dozen dead sons
frozen in place by men
who should have known
that anger is hereditary
& seeking forgiveness a sin

## Dogsbane

I have found God      in strangers      who spit
in my mouth      in the love      of men

I don't know      the names of      poorly made
decisions      my twenties      images of you

at the end of a fight   between us in a bathroom   at a house party
at a funeral      seeing two men cry      I have found God

haemorrhaging      the face of a man      beaten to death
on the street outside      my house      in the small hours

I have found God      drinking wine      in the car park
at four a.m.      under unlit streetlights      pissing in the dark

pretending      to be sober      so the cops leave us alone
hiding      in a church      out of fear for their lives

erasing the man      out of me      a hammer
in the back of my head   there sits   a bouquet of flowers

given to me      as an act      of retribution

18

in the hands      of men      feigning to be loved

I have found God      I have found God      I have found God
doing ninety-six      on the motorway      asleep at the wheel

# Mezerion

your cock is as hard as my life
& I have been struggling lately.

In my bedroom, we tell each other
this is just one time. Then one
of us will mistakenly think it isn't,
leaving it in the room
like it was an accident we can
make light of in the future.

It isn't & this is.

We will roll over back to back,
both scrolling on our phones
with after care as an afterthought
in the aftermath of the words that sit
fatally in the room.

You know I have been struggling
recently & tell me that this
is what we both need, like your cock
is medicine, & slipping it in my mouth

will cure me.

We both know my problems are financial
& that if you wanted to save me, you could
slip money in my wallet but you don't want
to make this one-off transactional.

& I don't want to make this one off
more than it needs to be, a transaction.
Mistaken words that have sealed the fate
that this is our last night on Earth together.

Tomorrow you will go back to being straight
& I will pretend I don't know what your come
tastes like. We have lost tonight in our mouths,
spitting the rules across the room.

# Dittany of Crete

Mother is a language you have never learned
                I hold the tongue & weep fierce sugar
this is censorship  undulating & gold (we keep secrets here)

If I were born with a womb I too would sew it shut
there is nothing but madness here
hereditary means to find loss eventually
            This patchwork hand-me-down of wrongful acts
fill the hands of men that know violence to be synonymous
with care

we were afraid of what came next
what your name could have been
     in the right temperature        under the right circumstance

## Spruce Pine

In summer heat so oppressive it carries handcuffs,
my mother tells me I am her son. The evening shaped
like a fist; my father breaks the doorframe & unloads
a lifetime of unanswered prayers into anyone who will listen.
He tells us            family is a knife forced into your hand.
My mother scurries into a corner,
a breadcrumb trail behind her.
She whispers            you are my son,
scooping me up in butterfly wings.
The heat tapers as months drift like clouds into autumn
& the sun rises too late – here he is a war machine,
bludgeoning into life. Practising heresies in the bathroom mirror
before repeating them in the hallway.
                        You can't use the knife,
he says                 but if you don't they'll kill you with it.
My mother, a shoebox of memories, talks the violence out of him,
ushering him into a perfumed room.
                        You are my son,
she says                you are not his.
In the aftermath of an accident, we give the children names;
mine has always been an apology.

# *Whin*

I am sold as a man
to anyone who will listen
to anyone other than me

in the sweatshop pub
across the road from my house
two men exchange awkward glances

as they look up into my window
& see me dancing obnoxiously loudly
to 'Pink Pony Club' by Chappell Roan

in tight Levi jeans
& a camp black string vest
with ankle high cowboy boots

a faux fur coat
a necklace gifted from a collection of friends
& black snapback that says 'in dog years I'm dead'

I hope those men
know that I look fabulous

that I feel fabulous

& that I could fuck
them & their dads
if I wanted to

# Dahlia

'I have insomnia' – words that you use to explain why the bags under your eyes look like they hold enough to feed a family of four, for the month. You don't have insomnia, you tell people that you do, and they give you that 'right-head-tilt' thing and say 'nawhh, it'll get better, buddy' or 'my friend actually has a really good tip it's blah blah blah' or 'maybe you're stressed? What are you stressed about?' – and you say "I'm not stressed" and though you are stressed, that is not why you have insomnia. To keep up appearances, you tell the doctor you have insomnia, you know that you don't but you tell him anyway because that's much easier than admitting (and addressing why you actually can't sleep). He offers to give you pills but you say "Well, the pills knock me out but they never really make you feel rested, y'know?" and he nods his head like 'yes, I am aware of what they do, buddy, I am a doctor but short of you actually addressing the issue, this is the best I can do'.

People start saying you look like shit more often than they say you look great or even good. That could be the fact that you are in your early thirties and possibly have 'early-onset alcoholism' but maybe you just like a drink on the weekend, at this point, it's difficult to tell. All you really know is that you need to get more sleep or, alternatively, kinder friends.

You know why you're up in the early hours – though you have no idea why you keep getting up at seven, you don't have an alarm set, or even a job to go to, but you think it might have something to do with the driving traffic that paces outside of your bedroom window, and the fact that you only have single glazed windows because moving into a cottage was an idyllic throwback to where you imagined you would live as an adult… as a child. But this is the city, and though you still have that countryside cottage dream, single glazed windows and a leaky roof is realistically the closest you are going to get till you get a 'real' job, and stop asking strangers off the internet to buy the products of your latest hobby. Though, to be honest, you really are quite good at making things, and sales are definitely up this last quarter, and you know it's not your parents because they don't know how to use PayPal, and honestly probably haven't thought about you in the last half-decade.

You tell people you're a night owl, you say "Hey, it's all good, I'm a night owl anyway" and they give you that sort of side smile and singular bounce head nod that says 'okay, buddy, because you look terrible, and my kids refer to you as the stinky plasticine man'. They might not refer to you as that but, if they were to refer to you as that, you wouldn't be surprised.

Insomnia doesn't let you do things like a regular person, and though this isn't insomnia, well, not really, it still looks and feels that way. So, things like showering, breakfast, thinking, tidying, sleeping (and that's a big one – probably the main one, really), lunch, working, moving, you know, regular people things, well, you can kiss them goodbye. You're still you, but the 'I haven't slept well in three months' version of you. Which is to say, not a version of you that is very good at anything. Still, you can walk the walk and talk the talk, and tell people you've got it under control, and they, after a little while stop asking anyway, so, in the long run, it's all good.

What you really need to do, and I mean really need to do, is focus on yourself. You hear echoes of 'try yoga' or 'meditation got me through it after the kids' or 'don't drink caffeine ever', and those are probably good ideas, the real issue is that you need to stay off your phone. I know, I know, it sounds so simple when you put it like that but it's only at 'awful o'clock' in the morning, when the rest of the team have gone to sleep that you can use the work account (the one that, for some reason, though you haven't worked there in two years, you have not been logged out of) to look at what your family is doing. You haven't spoken to them in four years, five this Autumn, and though you have no intention of breaking that silence now, you still like to see what they have been up to, how your brothers are doing, what your mum's health looks like (it was pretty rocky when you left and appears gravelly still). And you can't run the risk of accidentally throwing hearts in their direction from your own account lest you lose face in this dwindling battle of egos. Besides, you know that they aren't doing the same to your account, last time you saw them, they handled their phone like they were kneading dough and called 'memes' 'me-mes', so the likelihood that much has changed as technology has got smaller and more complex, and they have got older and more... old is, well, unlikely.

The obvious answer is to set up an additional Instagram account so that you can look during the day but with that sort of unfettered access, you wouldn't get anything done, day or night. And, you might feel like apologising to them, trying to pick up where you left off, you know, 'real water under the bridge' the whole situation, and that just wasn't an option, not after what they did.

Perhaps the more obvious answer is therapy but it's not a real problem yet, well, it's not a real problem that you are prepared to have to pay for yet, at the very least. Right now, it's just good ol' fashioned 'reminiscing', and quite frankly, that's where it can stay.

The last people I said "I have insomnia" – were the people at the jobcentre, and they looked me up and down like I'm an addict. At this point, I think I might be. They say that I need to get some sleep (like I haven't been trying that already), and settle in for some work. KFC is hiring – and that would be a great role for you, with your master's degree from, at the time, a top twenty university (though it has slipped in the years since you left, it was still pretty good when you were there). You tell them that you will do your damndest, and they look at you like you have just spat on their newborn son.

I know, I know, this is getting out of hand but, ironically, you can't afford to fix it till you're working, and you're not going to be working till you're sleeping better, and you won't be sleeping better till you address the issue, and thus, the cycle continues...

# Red Columbine

I am lost        somewhere      not knowing         your loss
in the weight    of knowing       understanding      my loss

I see you        around the way  against the current  your loss
in the water     struggling    trying to make sense of  my loss

I hold back    from growing    he flowers in my hands  your loss
mountains    stop them dead  as an act of forgiveness  my loss

a hostage      in a church       settling for man       your loss
finding faith  looking for God    in stained windows    my loss

# Ash Tree

I follow the outline of your shadow
with my teeth, playfully nipping at the parts
that stick out. You laugh like thunder
rolling down a mountain & I know I am
safe here. On bad days, when we fight,
storms break the treeline & I fear for
the villages below. I know we will save them
if we have to but we shouldn't have to. I wish
we could roll across centuries to find peace.
On good, slow nights, when the summer wind
finds your face, & the harvests made below
match how we feel above, I lose myself
in whirlpools; sea foam spluttering from your
body tastes like salt & I wash it into my skin.

We have never known urgency & find
our time to flow like seasons, unabashed
& constant. Your love, a falling petal,
blood sacrifice, & construction. I found your body
in an hourglass, playing with the sand on my fingers,
counting each grain till I had built you from dirt.
You found my body in water, washing in

the churn until I was whole, sewing me together
with vines.

We are the embodiment of love, all of it.
Forged together on an outcropped rock.
Two jade statues of Gods.

## Aspen Tree

I look for you in the sunset
hoping that somehow
you might come back.
& though you won't,
I still hold on to these rosaries
like they're supposed to be
all the secrets that you told to me.
& explosively, I call out at the sky,
counting dead stars on soft nights
that let soft cries bleed into the sun
like some sorts of sacrifice
are worth dying for.
But we've got these lies enforced
on to our skin, somehow it's better
to let that sink in than let whatever
truths may bring ring out in our lives
because the truth is, you didn't have to die.
There is no grand plan that involves
you not being here, no secret society
rising to power now that you aren't with us,
no reason to this madness, no rhyme
to this blackness that sits in every waking

evening & sees kin less deserving
going about their day.
It is so easy to get angry at you
demanding that you answer sets of questions
like we are still sitting in my bedroom
chatting shit till the people in the next room
hammer on the walls as we're laughing too loud.
I am so proud to have been your friend
for sixteen years, & though these tears still fall
on a daily basis I have to face it that you're
never coming home.
I will always watch the sunrise on the longest night
for the tradition that we started
& though our lives may have parted ways,
these days, we make art in your name.
A gift to you, like kissing the ring of the
last sovereign king of Canterbury.

This is my gift to you, the last sovereign king
of Canterbury.

## Bay Leaf

after a night out
all the stars
look like streetlights
guiding people you danced
with to late night buses
you count the windows
still awake
& try to remember who
you used to be before
any of this
happened to you

## Peach Blossom

I am soft in all the wrong ways
my body is limp, my cock is limp
& I am limp, laying there
breathing – in short, shallow graves.
                              Just like that
the worst words domino out of you
                              is it me
I croon out a              no
because I mean no
because yes is too dense
to wrap my mouth around
& though yes is what got us here
it is a false reclamation of youth
& we are getting too old to lie
about what we are

## White Lilac

to the sleeping man by my window   cowering in the heavy nights
leaning on the frosted glass        beneath a shriveled vacancy sign

this concrete is a mass of knocked teeth the winter writhing like snow
I found glass in your jaw              iced to stop the bleeding

life on the pavement              this is his burden
inches from recovery              you are mine

we set the house on fire    burning in the skin of our ancestors
& sleep outside together              in the cold wet snow

torn gloves & hot tea              slashed to ribbons
I pick glass from your mouth   under the aggression of the stars

we both look like mistakes         holding up statues
furrowed in his brow         to the Gods we have forgotten

underneath the window              covered in sores
lay two bodies              collapsed in the pierced air

## Lupine

I pour water from my bottle
& tell you this is Mercury
showing us how hot we are,
high we can get. Two faggots
in the city pretending to be other people.
I am dressed in hand-me-downs
from 'settled down' gays
& you are Diana Ross
with a feathering beard.
I want to be glamorous, I want
to be gorgeous; a mosquito full of blood.
You belt out a high 'e' in the back of a cab
& the driver pulls over ordering us to walk;
his shotgun mouth already reloading
as we readjust our skirts & scurry away
like field mice. We are high under the stars
            two burnt out lovers looking for anointment
            looking for a priest to put us on our knees.
I pour heroines from your mouth to mine till cessation.
Your cherry lip gloss; stolen from a stranger's bedroom,
is smeared around the tip of the bottle & tastes
like raindrops in the summer. In the evening

all the stars look like mistakes, scratched out answers
falling from the sky. We wait to catch them,
tell them, they're a dozen lies before we throw
them back into the night. The closest we have ever been
to meeting God is when we draw blood
from each other like a kiss placed upon a grave.

## Mint

come let your anger out on my body
  I will hold us (both)               together

prove I am not God – that we are not God
  I will hold us (both)              together

I found you under my fingernails
  sacred & alone

I spread your mouth away from youth
  turning your voice in my hand

when no one is looking
  I place it in my pocket & promise
to keep it safer than anyone else could

# Dead Leaves

There is enough lint in the dryer
to build a monument to you.

I found your hoodie
in the closet
   your face still
pressed against the sleeve.

I walk around the house
finding relics of what we
were before.

& think that there was maybe
more I could have said
before you left.

Our mattress is a poem
rewriting itself each morning
   how I can't sleep
without you, woven
into the lines.

# Bilberry

wear the skin of the mother wolf    call her names
*bitch    skinflint            construction    temple*

empty her drawers    replace them with flowers
*apologies    rectify            severance    adherence*

                    two sons warring
                    their father's absence
                    stapling chest hair medals

I describe absence as loss describing loss

a mother is a wind chime striking notes
that you are home    here she is
              still striking
              still gilded    like gold is only for statues

sacrifice    worshipping at the cunt of another woman

still bloodied    still waiting to be born    unsure how to breathe


finding wolf-child skin & tearing it from the walls
        this plea posturing as aggression
        is an unsharpened knife
        drawn against the neck
        of anyone who gets too close

# Laburnum

```
a t I w
 s o j i
  a a u l
   n n s l
    o y t f
     p o h o
      e n o r
       n e p g
        ll e i
         e i t v
          t s h e
           t t a u
            e e t s
             r n t
              i h
               n e
                g c
                   a
                    g
                     e
                      d
                       b
                        i
                         r
                          d
                           s
```

# Lemon Blossoms

the torn pages of your smile
leave paper cuts on my fingers.
I suck the blood from them
& tell you how I love you regardless.
There is no hate between us
even when we hate each other.
The undercurrent of love keeps our hands
from forming fists.

       We were born inside each other;
embryos that shared a face,
separated by different mothers,
always just a street away.
We kissed each other as strangers.
My legs are yours, my body is yours
I worship at the altar of your cock
& use my hands like a prayer
like what we are doing is religious,
like what we are doing is Godly.

       We are two angels, splayed out
across a bed, whispering history
to the cotton in makeshift forts
stitched for lovers, held together by distance

& all the things we could never tell
anyone else.

# Vine

This ██████████ will take longer to write ██████████████
I wanted to say that I ██████████ you. I don't know if that is true
yet but I am getting there ████████████████You have let me
down so many times ██████ & ██████████ this time is the last
time ████████████████████ ████████████████ ██
████████████████ ████████████████████ ██ I was free.
██████████ It's been several years ████████████████ ████
██████ since we last spoke, ████████████████████ ████
& ██████████ how could I let myself turn into you. ████████
I started to get better, ██████ I stopped listening to you. ████████
felt amazing ██████ ████████████████████ I don't hate you.
██████████ couldn't be you anymore. ████████████████ made
mistakes. ████████████████████████ I forgive you,
██████████████ You protected me ████████████████████
had to grow up ████████████████████

# Cardamine

make your mother proud // burn down the house
they found you in // this is not a rehearsal //
hide out in the smoke // breathe deeply // wait till the sirens
pass // sharpen your teeth // dive // your face is a window //
there is no one on the other side // this is not a rehearsal //
you pool water from the engines // measure yourself
against the plumes // hold yourself in place // drive nails
home // tell them he is still in there // watch your mother
cry // tell her // fire cleans all things // count your happy memories //
on fewer fingers // this is not a rehearsal //
build a monument // here lies // the body of your father // a man
is found in the ash // the evening is orange // baggy red faces
pressed up against your own // looking through // open your mouth //
use your fresh teeth // chew the words your mother told you //
this is not a rehearsal // fall // break your knees on the soft grass //
refuse to be picked up // cry // scrape off the burns // put your hands
in your pockets // watch the ambulance // take away the man
you could have been // tell your mother you are sorry // let down //
this is not a rehearsal // count the years against the sky //
make your mother //
proud //

# Pennyroyal

I suck the tip of my vape
like it is a cock,
inhaling the vapor
deep, down my throat,
& into my lungs.

I am wearing an oversized
hoodie – hiding my corse
from negligent eyes,
careening into my chest,
trying to spot whether
they should find my jawline
attractive or not, looking
for any indication
that I might be prey,
hoping they can explain
the rigidity building
across their bodies.

I am clean shaven
a hat pulled down low
like I'm a superhero hiding

in every Marvel movie.

Mullet blowing in the wind
headphones in, listening
to aggressive men
screaming instead
of speaking to therapists..

Here I am safe
unafraid of the hounds
across the street
ogling my tongue
as it runs the length
of my cherry-flavoured
vape.

I turn a corner
& a pub sprawls out
across the pavement
a fight has broken free.
I dart my head down
quick as a gunshot
& move to enter a bookshop.
Within seconds, I hear
'oi' cracking across the sky

to the drumfire of bottles
working graves
into the concrete.

Out the corner of my eye
between the battle-worn
forty-year-olds trying
to save their pints
& twenty-something boys crawling
out the gutter, looking
for a knees up.

I see a storm of a man
maelstroming his way through
a crowd of misaligned outdoor seating.

He walks up to me,
squares his eyes around my chest
& grunts. Letting out a roar; cymbals
crashing from an overzealous
fan misjudging a spin kick
in a mosh pit & absolutely
nailing the drum kit.

He takes the two fingers

he's put inside his wife
for the last thirty years
& presses me in the chest
like a stiff breeze in January.

The boys, kids really, circle like hyenas
ready to chase me down.
The squall of a man raises a hand
& the pups retreat to their cages.
"Where did you get that hat?"
the cyclone says to me.

"internet" I reply, my voice
cracked like a thrown plate.
"internet he says" he says
raising the temperature
of around him.

"I like it" he says.
"Going to get me one
just like it".

This man has known fear,
seen it paraded across the face
of everyone he has ever spoken to.

He sees it now, across from him,
on my face, in the way my body
has closed down; quietened.

He says "thanks" & leaves
like a sudden downpour
extinguished by the heat
of the sun.

I climb back to where it started,
raising my hands like cockcrow,
fumbling for my vape,
keeping my tongue locked
to the roof of my mouth,
out of fear of my own voice.

I look towards the bookshop
I avoided so narrowly
due to luck as good
as my credit score.

My body, two fingers heavier;
two extra ribs grown
to protect me
from careless men;

planted like oak trees
hundreds of years ago
in first bloom, minutes
after I needed an acorn;
ready for when I next need a forest.

Stained in the bellicosity
of the afternoon, the bookshop,
a few feet away, could have been
intercontinental.

I walk in & watch
as the eyes surge over me
checking for wounds
– reminding them of their own.
Wanting to ask if I was okay
but unsure of what language
to use. Any would have done
I would have responded to anything,
if someone had asked.

But they didn't & I didn't speak.
I just looked at books of poetry
not reading the names. Not looking

at titles. Waiting for time to pass
like a slow novel, quietly closing a chapter.

I walked to the door,
looking back like they do in films
at the swathes of people
that had watched me come in
frightened & alone, & would watch me
leave frightened & alone.

That night, when I was in my room
the curtains drawn to a close.
I would peel the clothes off of me,
ball them in a fist & pray
for my beard to grow back.

In my wardrobe, I threw out
everything that would hide my body
& remembered how to smoke.

# Belladonna

Your sister, a gentle web
told me that you
are afraid of the dark.
I told her that I, too,
am afraid of what's out there.
She said that's not what she meant.
You are afraid of the dark.

Your sister, a cut eye
told me that you
are afraid you will go blind.
I told her that I, too,
am afraid I will lose my sight.
She said that's not what she meant.
You are afraid you will go blind.

Your sister, a shivering glass
told me that you
are afraid.
I told her that I, too,
am afraid.
She told me that's not what she meant.
You are afraid.

# Traveller's Joy

coming out is like meeting God
        in the kitchen at four a.m.
        a cast iron skillet in its hand
        raising above your head
ready to smite the only non-believer
in the room

but you catch your soft jaw in a reflection
put down the skillet      cradle your face
& offer it as a sacrifice
        to the ceiling light
        to the hard edges
        you've made
to your parents

somewhere in a backlit room where
no one knows your name      they rejoice
& drink sweet nectar like shots
        celebrating
        that your wait
        is finally over
a new life has been born

## Purple Lilac

Was that a pencil or a stick behind his ear? You would think it was a pencil, what with this being a class and all but with Smithy you could never be too certain. He was a weird guy, that's for sure but I think that is why I liked him so much. He had long rolling curls that shaped his face in the same way a frame shapes a painting. Piercing blue eyes that looked like the bottom of a pond, and a gap in his front teeth you could drive a coach through.

"Aye, yo, Smithy, what you saying, bud? Pub lunch?" – Now, I know that Smithy doesn't drink, not since the accident, but the pub round the corner from class just got a new 'gastro-menu' to go with their new 'gastro-chef', their last chef, Bill, retired and has since taken up drinking full-time. "Aye, bud, yeah, bud, I'm thinking I might give it a miss, bud" – man, that gap was huge, big enough to house a family of four even. "Alright, bud, alright". Looks like I'm drinking alone, well, eating alone, I'm never drinking alone, not because I've got loads of mates, just because I don't want to turn into my dad, and pub lunches in the middle of term is how he started, well, according to my mum, not that I've seen her in a while.

I grab my bag and head toward the door. Shuffling people shuffle out of the room in an orderly fashion, well, orderly enough. I let them pass, and see Smithy waiting at the front desk, clasping his fingers, his face reddening and then relaxing, sort of like he was practicing for the 'holding your breath' world record, which, to be fair, he could have been like I said, he was a weird guy.

"You alright, Smiff?" I say. "Alright, bud? Yeah, bud, I'm alright, bud, just got to talk about something." – I'd not really noticed it but he says 'bud'... a lot. I say "Yeah, okay, I'll catch up with you later, yeah?" "Later? Yeah, bud, sounds good." And then I left.

Walking through the corridors, the grey stucco walls making this learning establishment look more like a prison than an educational centre, I wondered what was up with Smithy. Now, like I keep saying, he's a weird guy but there's weird and then there's 'blacking out from lack of oxygen whilst you wait for your lecturer to finish shuffling papers' weird, not that he did blackout but I think if I hadn't spoken to him, he probably would have done.

I always think about what attracts me to the 'weird guys', there was 'Bryan', who got really upset if you pronounced the 'Y' like an 'I', which apparently I only ever did when he and I were arguing, and he felt it was to wind him up purposefully, honestly, I could never tell the difference. He and I were only together for a couple of months, it just felt like an eternity. I was happy when he decided to join the navy. Also, it meant that I could tell my friends that I dated a squaddie, and that led to all sorts of conversations about whether or not I ever saw his 'cannon balls'.

Then there was 'Stacey', and Stacey was a weird one as she was the only girlfriend I had ever had, and I was the only boyfriend she had ever had, and realistically, we were the only straight sex that either of us had ever had, back when we were teenagers, and trying so desperately hard to fit in. It's kinda funny looking back at it, the only two gay kids in class would end up hooking up to prove they're not gay only to break up because, lo and behold, they are gay. She was sweet, and I think about her from time to time. I thought about looking her up recently but back when we were kids, she was always harping on about changing her name to something more romantic, like Anabelle or Siren or something, so I didn't bother.

I wanted Smithy to be different though, I liked that he was a weird guy, in fact, it was his 'weird guyness' that attracted me to him in the first place. He was always saying or doing something that made you think "what the Hell was that?" like the time I walked into his bedroom and he had a lightbulb in his mouth with a broken, exposed extension cord wrapped around his chest, that he was trying to turn on with his right big toe. And when I asked him what he was doing, he looked serious and said "Er, I'm just trying something out", like what he was doing was the most obvious thing in the world, and I was the fool for not understanding exactly what was going on in this 'Battista-esque' suicide attempt. But he said he was fine, he was always fine, he had been a little less fine after the accident but he had assured me since that he was once again 'fine', and that I shouldn't worry about him, and that worrying was a waste of imagination, and that I should imagine better things like dogs with jetpacks, or house prices dropping.

I wanted Smithy to be 'the one', you know? Like you see in films, or, to a lesser extent, daytime television adverts where they talk about how important it is to have life insurance if you're over fifty. They have those really happy couples that are all smiles and nice teeth, looking really positive as they start tucking money away so their family won't have to suffer the crippling financial burden of buying them a wooden box to be buried in when they die… and all for just four pounds a week. I think he could be, at least to me, he could be my 'the one', and I think about telling him this from time to time, telling him that I love him – not that I have ever told anyone I loved them, well, and meant it. I think I might have told that to my parents, back when I was a kid but my memory was pretty hazy. My therapist says it's probably all the trauma but I think I just didn't have any memories with remembering, maybe that's the same thing.

I'm thinking, I'll grab him a coffee from the cafeteria and wait for him after his meeting, or whatever the Hell it is that's he's doing. Then I'll tell him I love him and he's going to tell me he loves me too, and then we are going to go back to my place – his place is almost always gross, and we are going to fall asleep in each other's arms watching some shite film about mutagenic animals attacking cities, and it is going to be, just as it is meant to be.

The queue in the cafeteria is out the door and down the hall, so I settle for one of those vending machines that have drinks and snacks from brands you've never heard of like 'Jazz Apple – peach iced tea with mint' and 'Pempsi'. I get him a 'Pempsi' and start heading back to the classroom. Outside, the sky has opened up and is letting an entire ocean fall down, the only reason I bring that up is that Smithy lives so much closer to campus than I do, and he is going to want to go to his as it's 'more efficient' – cleaning the damn place would be 'more efficient' but whatever. So, I start to rethink my plan, maybe I'll tell him I love him another day, maybe the rain is an omen, a bad omen, specifically. Maybe this is fate trying to tell me he doesn't love me back or we're not ready to say this to each other, maybe he's not ready, maybe I'm not ready? I think I am, I am pretty sure. My uncle John, bless his soul, told me that when you know, you know, y'know? And I know, or at least I think I know, y'know?

Outside the classroom, I sit on a chair, a wooden thing that was made in the nineteen fifties for kids with much straighter backs than my own. And I wait for Smithy to finish, it's already been ten minutes since I left him in the first place, another ten go by, and another. I get up, peek my head through the door, and see Smithy awkwardly gesticulating towards a stack of papers on a desk, and the lecturer looking down sort of shaking his head. Whatever they were talking about was not looking promising for Smithy. Another five minutes pass and I hear the door creak open. I jump up, and Smithy is standing there, I push a bottle of Pempsi into his hand and say "thirsty?" with a twinkle in my eye that said "if you're not, I sure am, let's get gone". He looks at me, and says "Look, bud, I'm real sorry but I can't hang out for a while. I got an extension, and I gotta get this work good, you understand, right, bud?" – And yes, I did understand but that didn't change the fact that now I have to walk home in the rain, by myself, and the only cock that's running through my hands this evening will be my own. Maybe this, all of this, *is* a sign, the rain, Smithy not being free, Hell, the bottle of 'Pempsi' sticking out of Smithy's pocket to the left (classically meaning stop) as opposed to the right. Maybe we aren't ready for this, maybe *I* am not ready for this. What is love anyway? Just a couple of people that want to hang out, occasionally naked together, until one of them 'pops their clogs?' – I never understood that expression. Anyway, I say, 'Yeah, bud, I understand'. Yeah, I understand real good.

As I started walking away, the pouring rain doing its best to wipe any imagined smirk off of my face, something in me clicked, you know? I just, in that moment, realised, everyone I have ever seen in love, my parents, Uncle John, those happy couples in the death adverts, all of them, that happiness, that *love* was an image. It wasn't a real thing, no, the real thing, that lasted forever, right? It certainly wasn't scripted to sell 'what ifs' and make kids believe you were into each other.

I'm not ready to say 'I love you' to Smithy. I don't think I am ready to say it to anyone, maybe I never will be. Maybe I just need to wait for the right person, someone that doesn't electrocute themselves, or isn't a gay woman, and doesn't run off to the navy, or any other slew of different reasons to leave.

It's funny, isn't it? The way life tricks you like that? Gets you ready to take the biggest step in your life, and then, just as easily, takes that away from you. And, instead, makes you realise that you shouldn't have stopped seeing your therapist quite as quickly as you did, and maybe you should go back to Dr. Grace's office, and tell her that, like always, she was right.

Right now though, it's time to put the keys in the door, strip down to just my boxers, and thank whatever God I subscribe to that I did my shopping this week. All this so that I don't end up drinking alone, slowly turning into my father.

## Monthly Honeysuckle

& though we may not seize the day
in lover's storm or gentle kiss.
Remember, I will see your face
when all the world is set to break.
& if you thought the heart may miss
or come apart at start of day
know that I am here is as whole
in ardent bliss & take your hand
as right of way.
For when the light starts to abate,
& your smile is left adrift
know that I will mark your way
for only then can love exist.
Sometimes we are lost, or rarely found;
if the world does turn away
just know that I will hold this ground
till your legs begin to sway.
& when they drop, as mine will too
& our pulse starts to decay,
know that I will love you true
until the silent pass of day.

## Green Locust Tree

when I sit by the flowers
someone left
on the seafront
running my fingers
along the stems
pretending it's hair
following the shape
of your face in the mess
of petals

I find scents of you
asking to be exhaled
returned to the body
they once came from

## Wormwood

There are storms older than you
still howling at the sky
that know your name
make sure the concrete knows it too
this violence     a door painted shut     a suitcase
of your late father's belongings     ground to dust

       rest your head on your arms
       the night has already taken
       so much

for you     there is nothing more to find
regardless of what you are looking for

                   he is gone

on the ocean     where you sold your tongue
to any man who would take it
sits a heavy word               your name

                   forgiveness

scratched on a piece of wood
& used to beat you to death

find your body dashed against the rocks & ask why
you hid it there in the first place
not everybody was meant to bloom
not everybody was meant to survive

# Rosebay

The first time you kissed, was on a worn sofa
in your best friend's dad's house. Your best friend's dad
was asleep upstairs & you were learning the anatomy of young men
  through your fingertips,           boys            really.

It was July.
It had been July for months.
You were holding on to your birthday before the shade
of autumn guzzled you into winter & ate the man out of you.
A man that your best friend's dad would recognise.
Your own father would release you like pulled petals in the wind.

Your mother often called you *'petal'* because of the perfume you
wore. Your dad said perfume was for faggots & you apologised
through cold beers. He washed his hands off you before every
supper & sharpened his apologies on the corners of your face each
morning.

At the end of July – you would be eighteen; a small stone in a vast
sea. You would walk out in the brittle evening &, like a lost dog,
never return.

Your best friend's dad would ask you *how you became so lost?*
Together you would listen to the crickets weep, heavy &
unburdened,
as the summer gave in to dust.

As a kid, at your parent's house, a suitcase would be waiting, always
full, always heavy, always there. You would pick it up from time to
time to test its weight. One day, when it was finally lighter than
you, you picked it up, kissed both sides of it's cheeks, raised it above
your head, & threw it against a wall, spilling unnumbered years of
bruised apologies across the floor.

Later, when you had stuffed your fists back inside, & taped it shut,
an old man would unstaple his hands from his pockets,
place them on either side of your head like bandages,
& tell you that your mother was buried under the sunflowers
in the garden – still sleeping where he'd left her.
This would be the last time a body was shared
with a man you did not know.

## Nettle

they tell my father he has olive skin
which is why he sells knock-off clothes

|this is the eighties
(in the eighties) they remind him|

he is off-white          /off-brand
he is discounted         /reduced

a yellow sticker surrounded
by white stickers

they say your sons
will be golden too

the colour of piss

# *Crowfoot*

this vision
a heavy
burden

awakening
unrelenting
resisting

this feeling
in my body
urges to stop

awakening
unrelenting
resisting

this feeling
in my body
urges to stop

annihilating
everything
the quiet

# Harebell

I'm writing about grief because it's the only thing I have left of some friends. Well, I say that, I have the memories but they are stationary, static. I worry that if I think about them too often, they will change over time. Grief however, well, that grows with me, that's their place in my chest – and yes, I know that people say 'grief doesn't get smaller, we just grow around it' but I think it grows with you. It becomes another part of who you are, like a scar, it might pale but it doesn't stop being there. That being said, maybe there is some sort of surgery for grief. If there is, I am definitely too poor for it. Hell, I'm too poor for it even if it is just 'therapy'.

So, I live with the grief and it grows with me, and together we don't remember all my dead friends. We only think about them when we walk past places their memories haunt, old houses, streets I met them on, supermarkets, never my own house, the places we grew up together, every pub in a two mile radius, never my own house, gardens from here to the sea, both train stations, the bus station, but once again, never my own house.

I can't have them in my own house and I won't allow the grief to remind me they had ever been here. This house is for the living, for the future, and for the inaudible cries in the night when I hear them knock, asking me to stay safe, telling me to stay safe.

One day when I wash up on the opposite side of life, and they meet me, stating that I am earlier than they thought I would be (not through any intentional movement on my part, I am just accident prone), I'll tell them that I missed them, and they will tell me they could have waited forever longer if it meant that no one was going to miss me the way that I miss them.

They were good boys like that, always thinking of other people.

## Full-Blown Rose Placed Over Two Buds

Finding you was the secret eleventh track
on a ten track half-hour album that was, at the time,
inexplicably forty-five minutes long.
You were waiting for me thirteen minutes
into the encore. Hidden beneath an array
of silence &, if you listened real closely,
band members talking about how much they miss
their wives & girlfriends whilst they were on tour.
In the thudded quiet stapled to the back of the album,
that which no one would think to check, that which no one
would think to listen to all the way through without leaving
the album playing whilst they bathed or by some other
sort of accident. You hid, waiting for the opportunity to pour
your voice out on to me, swallow me in the depths of your throat,
drink my body through a CD walkman that skipped if you walked
too fast, even with anti-skip technology as advertised in all the
catalogues. This was before the internet, before everything was
found before it was released. This was when music was a hand-
me-down from our older brothers & sisters – back when Marilyn
Manson had his ribs removed to suck his own cock & Kurt Cobain
fans still cried on April 5th. Long before we knew each other by
the smell of the pillow or by how we liked our morning drinks.

This was when youth was something we all had & growing up
meant giving up & getting old meant being in our twenties. This
was when everyone we knew was a kid, our siblings friends, or
our parents that were nearing death by being in their forties. So,
when I heard your voice at thirteen, I felt I had waited my entire
adult life to understand what it meant to be loved by someone
outside of my family. Listening to your lyrics "And if you slit my
throat" made me understand what aduthood was "With my one
last gasping breath". & just like that I was known, I was yours, I was
no longer waiting to be found "I'd apologise for bleeding on your
shirt". Haemorraghing at the seams, I took your voice, my voice
still ungrown, & placed it in my mouth so that we might share the
same breaths, so that our lungs might inflate the same way, & when
I sang your mouth might move too, sharing our moments together.
My mouth eventually grew too large to contain the words you sang,
my body a ransacked temple to yours, starched in the familiar scent
of cigarettes & vodka from a night called 'Vodka Victims' that lived
up to its name in the town that I grew up in & grew out of. When I
turned eighteen, the oldest I have ever been, & likely, even with the
added years, the oldest I will ever be again. I found your voice had
grown into a tower, a monument forged in ash, divorce, & more
marks that were par the course. We would
always have secret tracks from back when we were kids.
You were mine & I was a dime a dozen.

## Yellow Acacia

The first boy I ever kissed had the smallest tongue
he kissed me so the girls would kiss too
I kissed him because loneliness is a hanging knife.

       I haven't known what to do
       with that feeling since.

So, I keep it as a knotted rope above my bed
placing my head through the loop
from time to time, to see if it still fits.

It smells like perfume left out in the sun,
& I am reminded of all the boys I have kissed.
All their tongues – & where they live on my body.
Heavy in my mouth – all these boys are hanged with me,
signposts marking how it is a crime to try to live.

# Tendrils of Climbing Plants

Sometimes I wait at the train station
to see if you will get on the same train
as me – even though you live
where I am departing from. Maybe you
will be waiting for someone else
on the train as it pulls in, maybe
you will be going to see another ex-lover.
Wouldn't that be a thing, for us
to see each other as strangers?
Strangers that know each other's secrets
but strangers nonetheless?
& wouldn't it be funny if we said hello?
& wouldn't it be hilarious
if we went & got coffee?          Maybe we
could talk about why we broke up &
maybe we could not shout this time.
& maybe we could walk the length
of the beach, & maybe get that drink
we said we would get when we could
look at each other again.          & maybe
I could pull out two tickets & you could
sit next to me on the train & we could

hold hands & remind each other
how warm the world can be.　　& maybe you
could tell me that you missed me,
& I could crack a joke, & you could ignite
the carriage with your laughter, & maybe we
could sleep like letters in envelopes
or tell each other new secrets,
no longer as strangers but as friends
or maybe we could not say anything
& that would be fine too. A very fine thing.
Wouldn't that be funny?

I've been waiting at the train station
twice a week for nine months.
I am yet to see you.
But I think it will be funny when I do.

# Bramble

love        bottom        p
    is a        less        it
hate        reck        ex


f                l                        kn
  illed with        ives we do not        ow
k                kn                        n


cur                        v                        sc
  sed is the        oice that        olds us
bles                        ch                        h

# Dark Geranium

I remember when uncle John told me about marrying Myriam, his first wife. He told me "Listen, it's all pretty straightforward, if you loved her, you married her, and that was that." – He coughed and sputtered through the 'and that was that' part, that's what forty years of smoking will do to you, although uncle John will tell you he has never been healthier, with a chuckle.

"It can't be that simple," I say, "You hardly knew Myriam, you met her the week before when you bumped trolleys in a supermarket", and it's true, uncle John had known Myriam a week before they got hitched, at least that's what dad told me, back when he and I were speaking. "Aye, but those trolleys bumping, well, that was fate, lad" – I always hated it when he called me 'lad', not because I wasn't a lad (though I wasn't, I was well into my thirties at this point) but because when uncle John said it, he sounded like a pirate, a sleazy pirate, but a pirate all the same. I could just imagine him asking me to climb the rigging, or whatever it was that pirates ask 'lads' to do. I often wondered if uncle John had been a pirate and that's why dad didn't speak to him either. It could, of course, just be because dad was a bastard to everyone up and down the country but it could also potentially be the pirate thing.

"Fate" I scoff. "What's 'fate' got to do with it?" "Everything", and he paused for a minute like he was reaching inside his own skull and trying to scoop out the memories into the bowl in front of him. "It has everything to do with it, boyo" – somehow that was worse than 'lad' but I couldn't tell you why. It also meant that uncle John was getting serious, 'boyo' only came out when he was going to tell you something of great importance… or if he was hammered, and judging by the room we were in, the time of day, and the nightdress he was wearing, I would argue it unlikely that he was plastered, not impossible mind, just unlikely.

Uncle John traced his face with the tips of his fingers, profiling his nose, and pausing over the various bumps, scratches, and scars that a man might get throughout his lifetime. "Fate is what holds us together, sure, we have free will but only on the small scale, only in the immediate, y'know?" and though I didn't, I nodded along like I did. "See, Myriam and me, we were always destined to meet, to bump trolleys, to romance, to marry, 'fate' had it all planned out for us. I wasn't sure when I saw her, what with the snaggletooth and all but as soon as I heard that laugh, well, that laugh could melt glaciers." Uncle John always fancied himself as a bit of a poet, he would remind us all, back when we were all still talking to each other, about how his poem was chosen for an anthology, and how well he did in his O-levels. "These hands were made for hard graft though, poetry be damned", and every time, without fail, when he said 'poetry be damned', you better believe that whatever was in his hand would meet the ground in a display of amateur dramatics. Me and the other kids would wait till the 'drunken boyo' came out at Christmas, and then ask uncle John about poetry. The number of times I heard my mother call from the other room "No, John, you're holding soup, we've just had the couch reupholstered!" or something to that effect. Classic.

"It can't all just be 'fate' though, surely? How did you know that you loved her or that you might love her?" – and I knew, as soon as the words had left my mouth, that this had been a mistake. "How did I know? How did I know? How do you know anything? How do you know that the wind blows or that gravity is real?", as he said the gravity thing, I think I may have flinched because he laughed, and uncle John had a great laugh, he used to say that Myriam had given it to him on her deathbed. And every time he said it, you could see his eyes well up a little bit, even his next wife, the dreaded 'Shirley' – who insisted you pronounced it 'Shar-lee' would watch and crack a short smile before her face returned to concrete, honestly, I never knew what he saw in her, and though I wasn't happy when she died because it meant that uncle John was alone again, I was a little bit happy that he could leave the house unchaperoned by a gaggling harpy.

"You know where I got that laugh from, don't you?" He said. "I know, uncle John, I know". He coughed out what must have been the last part of his lung into a balled fist, and looked at it as if to see if there was anything left that he could shove back in. "You'll get there, lad, you know that, right? You'll find your Myriam, you'll find her, and you'll just know, y'know?" and for the second time in five minutes, I didn't 'y'know?' but I smiled and bopped my head along to an invisible beat.

"Hey, why did you fall out with dad?" – I thought he might have shown up here today but I guess some things are thicker than blood. "Well, lad, that's a story for another time." – A pretty bold statement considering… "Is there anything you want me to pass on to him? Not in person, obviously but I can send him an email." And uncle John looked at me, a long look that read every aspect of my being, all of the stupid mistakes of my past, all the hopes and goals of my future, and the face of his nephew, that was here, now. "Tell him, tell him I love him, boyo, tell him that even after all this time, after all of this" he gestured, slow breathless movements about the room from his bed and then paused, waiting for his breath to crawl back inside. "Tell him that I still love him."

And like it was fate, he shut his eyes, a murmur ringing out of a machine, wires running along his arms, and into his chest, sparking to life rather ironically.

"I will, uncle John, I will."

## Yellow Rose

When you exploded on my chest in butterflies & red fire truck
moths you told me that I could not leave – that I must rust in the
bed
I have made. In the early years, I would have run. Legs
& fear – but, as the years have aged me like china, I stay.
I'll make hot tea, & we can laugh into old age. You
agree in glances of hammering rain & month-long comas,
insisting that *this* is just what love is – whatever this is.

Several years ago – when we met – in the sea – a crested wave
we agreed terms & I surrendered my arms, rested
my hands in yours & drank from your mouth till hours
marched into days.

Here I allowed myself to eat sweet nectar & skank
till the grass died underfoot. The evening light blissed,
cradling us both – ensuring we would never find our way
home.

As time ricocheted in tragic imbalance & your mouth grew
wide enough to hide secrets. I learned of gin-soaked rags in the
laundry

notes in mirror steam that left your number everywhere
but home with me.

We grew like yawns in the smothering darkness – oppressive &
distinct, a race to see who could find ourselves in the diaspora first.
    Neither of us knew how to wash home from our skin.
& neither of us could find our keys in the delicate night.

# Syringa

we tell each other lies to seem interesting  tell each other stories
from when we took drugs  that we still take drugs  that age hasn't
caught us yet  that we can still fuck & fight & live like we used to
in our twenties  that we still go out on benders  that we still pick
up whatever's left at three a.m.  that this one time  we battered an
enormous security guard for not letting us in  & we'd do it again
if we had to  that we are still young  that youth is an idea  that to
be young  you just had to think young  & who wanted to be like
that anyway  we talk about insurance policies  & what it's like with
the partner  & where we went on holiday this year  & where we're
going next year  & how we might adopt soon  & how we grew up
but never grew old  we tell each other about the mistakes we made
how me miss Josh & Matt & Kieron  how they were never going to
make it anyway  how it's better like this  how we miss them  & they
would have been great dads  how we knew all their secrets  how we
keep them now regardless  we tell each other about the good old
days  the days that are yet to come  the men we've loved  the men
we've lost  the men we're still with now  how we saw that security
guard again  how none of us apologised  how he didn't recognise
us  how he was fucking huge still  how we might have exaggerated
how we battered him  how we don't really take drugs anymore  how
we stopped drinking so much  how we want the boys to be proud

of us  how we all have gastro problems  how work is  how yes  we
are still in the same job from all those years ago but now  we're the
manager  how life is getting better  how we're surprised we made it
this far  how we're surprised any of us made it this far  we tell each
other how happy we are that some of our friends got together  how
they're having kids  how they got off the drugs  how some of them
are still on them  how many countries they've seen  how many years
we've all lived  how much we're saving for the future  we tell each
other lies about how well we're all doing  how this meet up once a
year is enough for each of us  how we couldn't do it more anyway
because we're all too busy for our friends  we tell each other how
expensive the divorce was  how it couldn't work after we lost the
baby  how it was probably for the best but we're totally fine now  we
give each other advice  say we're going to get through this  that if we
want to grab a coffee soon  we can make time  we say that we have
always made time  that 'anything always' extends both ways  that
we have a spare room  & if we need somewhere to stay  we can stay
with us  we laugh  & we say thanks  & we tell each other we should
do this again soon  we should do this again soon  we should do this
again soon  we should do this again soon  we should do this again
soon  we should do this again soon  we have each other's numbers
we should do this again soon  we should do this again soon  we
should do this again soon  & we part ways  & we say keep in touch
& we won't keep in touch  no matter what happens  that a spare
room is a success in this day & age  that we aren't a success in this

day & age  that maybe the boys got it right  that that was crazy talk
that we don't really think like that  that that is just a silly idea  that
we're fine  that we're fine  that we're fine  that we're getting there
that we'll be okay in a couple of days  that we just need a break  that
we just need a break  that we just need a break   that things will get
better  that maybe we will keep in touch this time  that next year
will be our year  that this is just a setback  that maybe things will
work out  that maybe things will work out  that maybe things will
work out  that maybe things will work out

# Palm

When they march against you
fingers & wars – drawing lines
on the shadow of your face,
aiming for the angles of your past.
When they tell you hereditary means
you will wash out in time. That time
is a flower & flowers are for picking.
When they cover your body in tar
& vinegar & say you have no place here.
Tell them that you have tasted the salt
from the sweat of dying & that it is
recognition. Tell them that you are
rolled R's & glottal stops – that their voice
holds no weight in your future, no movement
in your history – that your current is spoken
in languages they cannot understand.
When they bring you through
to white rooms saying your name
in their tongue & tell you
that, that is how it is pronounced. Spit.
Spit so hard you break teeth. Spit
till you fill an ocean & ask them how

many times they will drown here.
When they learn the dimensions
of your ancestors, the depths of your birth
when they learn why your hair curls &
your nose is crooked – break them. Feed them
your mouth in cursive – write them letters
in fury & concrete. Remind them
you have been here before, that you
will be here again, that your epithet
is a cemetery, that cemeteries are full
of people that look just like you,
that they are dying out. When they bring you
war, when they show you your delicacies
& tell you how they discovered them,
feed yourself sugar. Eat berries
that remind you of home, drink nectar
from cans & gorge yourself on the blood from your veins.
Eat sugar & sweetness & sing out in defiance.
You have earned respect even when you had to fight for it.
Your body is made of violence, your voice is a gun,
& your tongue is the trigger – waiting for you to fight back.

## Scarlet Nasturtium

we say we are wrestling
& your parents call us
gay till one of us passes out
in your bedroom
a bruised oesophagus
takes us to hospital
they say we were wrestling
the doctors look at us
experimenting across the room

# Convolvulus

Writing fanfiction about my own life
like I am anything other than ordinary.
This taste in my mouth is average,
We are two lost causes that have found each other
hidden away in a cave, wearing seaweed loincloths
& splitting teeth on rocks we cannot eat.

Instead, I write fanfiction where I pretend to know you;
man that sits across from me on the train to work
in the morning. Reading. A book. A newspaper.
Or listening to music, I have called you Daryl
because I have never named anything & we have
never spoken. & I am not good at telling you about
myself, what my name is. How I see you every morning
& how you always look a little sad.

Or, in this universe, I can pretend to know you.
We will know each other's names
& we hold our hands under tables at coffee shops,
so violent eyes don't see what love looks like.

# Wolfsbane

your unwashed cock forces me to gag in a dark room at the back of
the club        we have been dancing all night sweat & dirt &
alcohol you have drunk too much & I am on my knees with your
soft cock in my hands trying to encourage you to grow   you pull
the back of my hair into a fist & I chip my tooth on your eagle belt
buckle  you laugh I let out a cry & throw up down your legs      you
push me to one side pulling your jeans back up before walking back
out onto the dancefloor        I put the piece of false tooth back
in my mouth & order a tequila soda      this night has just started

# *Parsley*

The bedroom//is a battle//between two//warring factions
The washroom//is a warship//with a//dreadnought sinking
The dormitory//is a dominion//dining with//silent partners
The sittingroom//is a silioquy//spoken by//children playing
The chapel//is a cell//coddoling a//prisoner's face
The parlour//is a prayer//preying on//the weak
The theatre//is a tantrum//targetting the//gloating public
The galley//is a God//grieving the//lost lives
The lavatory//is a life//laying down//in ruins
The inglenook//is an idea//firing youth
The frontroom//is a factory//engulfing hands
The entry//is an emergency//aching years
The anteroom//is an album//yawning softly
The youngroom//is a yearning//quickly expunged
The quietroom//is a quote//untold here
The utilityroom//is an ugliness//vaguely lying
The vestibule//is a visage//jangling keys
The jailcell//is a joke//kicking doors
The keep//is a key//mostly bleeding
The mensroom//is a monitor//needing justice
The newsroom//is a nest//of hate
The operatingroom//is an occupation//releasing no-one

The recoveryroom//is a romance//holding weight
The hotelroom//is a home//xeriscaping land
The xrayroom//is a xylographer//zeroing out
The zincateroom//is a zone//broken down

# Cranberry

I am left with all the empty
bottles you used to keep
as souvenirs. I keep
trying to throw them out
but somehow they end up
on the kitchen counter
next to a stack of photos
of you & I.

If I throw them out,
you are gone
& I will have to learn
what comes next.

The hardest part of a breakup
is living through the grief
of knowing you can still see
them from time to time,
just not how you saw them
before.

I sold everything that reminded me

of you. I sit in an empty house
wearing nothing, holding nothing.
This skin, too delicate to take off,
is a keepsake sagging
in the places that knew your fingertips.

I want to reclaim the empty
that had once been shared
& tell myself I will be okay – that time will fix me,
knowing that if I bump into you in five years,
I will still remember the cologne you wore
when we told each other secrets.

*August 9th, 2008, Canterbury, England*

# Where The Flowers Grow

found yourself   somewhere          a lake or a river
raising me up
nearing the edge        at the bottom          with only your
hands    I would drown

I like to think you        ask for forgiveness        wondering where
I am  cradling a photo
lie awake at night        praying for sleep        how lost we both
are        what I could have been

a lake or a river  raising me up          I like to think you
ask for forgiveness
with only your hands    I would drown        lie awake at night
    praying for sleep

raising me up          I like to think you        ask for
forgiveness        wondering where I am
I would drown        lie awake at night        praying for sleep
    how lost we both are

I like to think you        ask for forgiveness        wondering where
I am  cradling a photo

lie awake at night      praying for sleep      how lost we both
are      what I could have been

ask for forgiveness      wondering where I am cradling a photo
praying for sleep      how lost we both are      what I could have
been

wondering where I am cradling a photo
how lost we both are      what I could have been

cradling a photo
what I could have been

I could have      been more than you      ask for forgiveness
   I like to think you
held onto that photo      in my fingertips      praying for sleep
   lie awake at night

wondering where I am a lake or a river   somewhere
found yourself
how lost we both are      with only your hands at the bottom
   nearing the edge

ask for forgiveness      I like to think you      wondering where I
am   a lake or a river

praying for sleep        lie awake at night        how lost we both
are        with only your hands

I like to think you        wondering where I am a lake or a river
somewhere
lie awake at night        how lost we both are        with only your
hands        at the bottom

wondering where I am a lake or a river  somewhere
found yourself
how lost we both are        with only your hands        at the bottom
  nearing the edge

a lake or a river somewhere                found yourself
with only your hands        at the bottom                nearing the edge

somewhere                found yourself
at the bottom                nearing the edge

found yourself
nearing the edge